Consider the Lilies

Mrs. God Poems

Also By Connie Wanek:

Bonfire
Hartley Field
On Speaking Terms
Summer Cars
Rival Gardens

Consider the Lilies:

Mrs. God poems

Connie Wanek

Connie Wanek (signature)

Will o' the Wisp Books
Bloomington, MN

© 2018 by Connie Wanek

All rights reserved.

ISBN-13: 978-1722080501

ISBN: 1722080507

Will o' the Wisp Books
2018

for mothers and daughters

CONTENTS

Mrs. God	1
Genesis, Cont.	2
Intelligent Design	3
First Love	5
The Beginning of Time	7
Peacock	9
The Impulse to Create	10
Day of Rest	11
Eve	12
Business	13
Martyrs	15
Ten Commandments	16
A Child	17
Peace on Earth	19
Hell	21
Yes	22
Complaint	24
Happy Birthday	25
A Sign	27
The Bright Side	29

Acknowledgments

Mrs. God

Someone had to do the dirty work,
spading the garden, moving mountains,
keeping the darkness out of the light,
and she took every imperfection personally.

Mr. Big Ideas, sure,
but someone had to run the numbers.
Then talk about babies: he never imagined
so many.

That was part of his charm, of course,
his frank amazement at consequences.
The pretty songs he gave the finches:
those spoke to his

innocence, his ability to regard
every moment as fresh. "Let's give them
free will and see what happens,"
he said, ever the optimist.

Genesis, Cont.

Other days God seemed severe,
but he was always hardest on himself.
Curious, he watched Mrs. God,
the way she distanced herself
from disasters. Especially the ones
he himself unintentionally set in motion.

All God asked for was eternal work.
Luckily something was always broken.
A virus began to kill all its hosts,
or claws needed sharpening, and afterwards
he had to make them retractable.
Weather was a challenge,

finicky, like those old carburetors.
But gravity turned out perfectly:
hummingbirds could fly, but people
didn't float around, and two legs worked fine.
Mrs. God's radiant smile, yes, he gave that
to the sun, and all the stars, and then to Eve.

Intelligent Design

Like someone from a small town
in the Midwest, Mrs. God
began, "I don't mean to be critical..."
God braced himself.

"...but honestly, the only thing keeping
a peanut out of the lung
is this little flapper.
I can understand that approach
in a toilet tank, but in Adam?"
"That's why I added
another lung," God explained.
"Mere redundancy? That's your answer?"

There were moments when even
The Couple grew exasperated.
She had already noted
the proximity of Adam's reproductive organs
to the terminus of his digestive tract.
"I'm not starting over,"
God said flatly.

And he didn't. After all, Mrs. God
had favored the centaur. Charming, yes,

but talk about duplication!
Sometimes eons had to pass before
they saw their mistakes
with any clarity. Luckily, God thought,
we have forever.

First Love

After God created love he felt
himself swooning. "What is this?"
he cried out to Mrs. God.
"What have I done?
Is it a kind of music?"
"It bears a strong resemblance,"
she said softly, watching the warm sea
begin to rise and fall, as though
longing for the moon.
"Take slow, deep breaths," she advised,
and it will pass."

But it didn't. All day God wandered
in Eden, on the verge of weeping.
The tree of the knowledge of good and evil
was in full bloom. He'd made it
self-pollinating, but now he changed
his mind and decided that to fruit,
a second tree must be planted nearby.
"Close, but not too close,"
Mrs. God, the horticulturalist, advised.
"The bees will find it."

Another evening, glorious among the clouds.
She was humming, mending something
when God touched her shoulder.
"Yes," she said, smiling. "Yes,
it was a good day."

The Beginning of Time

After a walk of indeterminate length,
Mrs. God pondered: "We need
a solid substructure so people can
organize their lives,
much as bones shape their bodies."
She had noticed that summers
felt a little short on Earth,
especially up north.

She asked, "Could we use light?
Sunflowers turn east every morning.
That's pleasant. And reliable. I could put
a sundial next to the birdbath."

"What about heat?" God offered.
"Thermometers mounted in the forest
and planted in the fields.
Breakfast at 60 degrees.
The bullfight could start at 82.
But if it stays cool, there'd be no fight."
That last thought was for her
and the children.

But much later
he found her asking the pines

how long they wanted to live,
and then came a terrible sadness.
Forever, they said in the wind.

And God declared,
though their countenance might change,
yet the pines would live
from the beginning of time
to the end.

Peacock

Mrs. God found the Lord at work
on the male peacock.
"It's sort of a joke," he said pleasantly.
He had, of all his animals,
the most joy creating birds

and the people who watch them.
Mrs. God thought he'd gone too far this time.
"Excuse me? Predators?"
"I thought we could make them poisonous,"
God offered. "Watch."

He breathed life into the peacock.
Mrs. God had seen this many times,
yet always she felt anxious,
searching the creature's eyes for light.
Ah, there it was!

Witnessing this made her acutely aware
of her own next few breaths.
Yet, as often happened, it was at that moment
that God began to lose interest
in what he hath wrought.

The Impulse to Create

God was the master
of excuses, as Mrs. God could attest.
He didn't need them; he just liked
to think them up. If truth
was a gray rock
he liked to add a dash
of bright orange lichen.

He extolled the virtues of frost
even as it blackened the dahlias.
All of Heaven was replaceable,
he maintained, as he excavated
the burn pit where he threw in
whatever he broke, when he worked
past exhaustion.

When he finally slept
his dreams could last for centuries,
and his daily chores fell
to Mrs. God, who had her own.
She loved him best sweet and drowsy
and tugged the clouds around him,
shushing the world.

Day of Rest

The good Lord had primer on his hands,
but paint could wait till Monday,
Mrs. God assured him, seeing how tired he was.

He said, "You should talk. You're still working."
It's true. She was wearing her garden gloves
and pants with muddy knees.

"Well, Eden's almost done for the season.
Bare ruined choirs in the arbor,
where late we walked."

"Choirs," he mused. "Is that a new word?"
She smiled. "How do you think
we should spell it?"

From a distance Earth was turning
into a masterpiece. God pondered a second
sun, so there'd never be a dark side.

"No," she reflected. "One noon is plenty,
and see how rich the blues are as light fades."
"Perhaps a moon then,

just a little one." And that
bit of tinkering was all they did
for the rest of the day.

Eve

"So that's what he likes," thought Mrs. God.
"You can hardly blame him."

He had practiced on many creatures,
perfecting certain features,
like the iris of the eye, distinctly floral,
and tears for that matter, adjusting the salt.

Adam had come first, of course,
and there were "issues."
"That tail has to go," Mrs God said.

So God began again with spare parts,
butterfly wings and peaches, a rib,
modesty. She would have a smooth gait,
he imagined, like a Tennessee Walker.

And actually her hoofs were Mrs. God's
only criticism. "But the hands," she said,

"You've done well there. Look at her
picking figs, just the ripe ones. So delicate...
wait till Adam sees her!" By this time, though,
God had almost forgotten about Adam.

Business

"I should have stepped in,"
God said, "when they began to barter
figs for sharpened stones."

"Don't blame yourself,"
Mrs. God took the Lord's hand.
"People are still basically good."

They looked down
as a cluster of speculators
began to short the new armistice.

"You gave them manna.
That was brilliant." She remembered
the day people realized this heavenly bounty

could not be seized, hoarded,
and monetized. From a distance
she had watched the most ambitious

struggle beneath insane burdens,
only to find swarming maggots the next
morning, their inventory spoiled.

One by one they seemed to catch on.
But eventually the very same people
invented hedge funds.

"Maybe we can learn something
from them," Mrs. God suggested,
"and just stop caring."

Martyrs

God thought martyrs were tiresome,
but he didn't feel he could say that.
As a group, they seemed like grinds,
inflexible, like students who would
do anything for an A.
Of course you had to respect
such serious people.

He felt perhaps their parents were to blame,
bearing all those children
so one could be sacrificed to the church.
The very word "sacrifice" had created
terrible misunderstandings.

"Consider the lilies," Mrs. God said
one morning, and that very phrase
became a refrain, calming and consoling.
It was midsummer, and lilies

were blooming everywhere in the fields,
their long buds springing open,
radiant, palms upward, arms wide,
none more beautiful than any other,
all surrendering to common joy.

Ten Commandments

After centuries of negotiation
in the manner of writer and editor,
God himself chose the stone and font.

"How many copies?" asked Mrs. God, patiently.
"I was thinking a thousand?" God answered,
sharpening his chisels. "At least for
the first edition. Some folks may need to share."

Mrs. God left him to it. The sound
of iron against rock grew faint.
She was shaping something milder,
a long, serious period of rain
across the outback, where such a gift
meant tears of gratitude.

Meanwhile God began to tire.
The commandments, formed letter by letter,
seemed wordy, even after he'd eliminated
most of the footnotes. His palms had blistered
without the gloves he always misplaced.
"Thou shalt not lie," he mused. "Or is it
lay?" She would know, if only she were here.

A Child

A child, said Mrs. God.
Must I? In some respects
foreknowledge was unbearable.
To wonder also meant to hope.

She tried then to imagine
a living spring
in the bed of a northern river:
what would someday be the Brule
in a place called Wisconsin
before that, too, passed away.

The spring looked like a small knot
in the sand, continuously loosened
by unseen forces, by many
invisible fingers,
small and restless as a baby's.

Water had a set of customs
within which incredible variation
took place. It was like
the flickering of starlight.

Perhaps there is no future,
and the mysterious unfolding

of the spring is all I can
truly be sure of, Mrs. God thought,
then in her ninth month.

Peace on Earth

Sometimes Mrs. God asked
simply to be called by her first name.
"It's the only thing that's mine
alone, she said, wandering
the Rosette Nebula, a wild place
that had immense potential
and was always burning and growing.

God had lately
created the black widow spider
that consumed her tiny mate
directly after he fertilized her eggs.
"That's not funny," said Mrs. God.

"I thought you would be pleased,"
he teased, "with the female's
proprietary ability to give birth.
What could be more vital?"

"Nothing," she said bitterly,
setting aside her observations
regarding the discomfort involved
in human reproduction.
"But if our goal is peace on Earth..."

"Peace on Earth," God repeated—
"Did we say that?"
"Many times."
God turned away.

God turned away,
as deep in the Heartland heavy snow
began falling, simple white,
and two bear cubs emerged,

wet and hungry, and took their first breaths,
while their mother groaned in her sleep.
"It could end like this,"
Mrs. God thought,
"except for those cubs."

Hell

"It's a thought," God said
when Mrs. God suggested that certain people
deserved to burn forever. "Are you
getting your rest?"

"You don't care enough," she accused.
"You care too much," he replied gently. "Tell me
what you mean by Hell."

All the punishments she described then
were already present on Earth
as it seemed no torture was beyond
human invention. The difference
was the word *forever*.

"Of course I do see," God sighed.
"Life began so simply, a few amoebas,
little brown sparrows, lovely people in a garden,
laughter on a summer night..."

"A romantic comedy," Mrs. God said. "Too bad
humans are addicted to drama."
"And explosions," God added. "Maybe
we could make Earth a dry planet,
no booze." And then, of course, he laughed.

Yes

People often prayed to Mrs. God
when they had requests.
They felt she would be kinder
and forward their petitions

sympathetically to the Lord
when he was most receptive.
She was like a village letter writer,
the soul with wondrous skills.

Yet it was actually God
whose default was "Yes, why not?"
He liked to see the children smile
even if bonbons spoiled their supper.

He liked the way a smoker's face
relaxed as she took a deep drag
after a hard morning.
He invented whipped cream.

"They won't thank you in the end,"
Mrs. God warned.
But he loved their ardent gratitude
even more than their faith,

the glowing face behind a royal flush,
a quick text in the night:
Baby here, all well, Mary resting, thx.

Complaint

God was annoyed.
"People think I'm responsible," he complained
as he watched them pulling
the bodies of children out of the rubble.
"Sometimes things just happen."

Mrs. God was holding back her tears.
But later she suggested they take
a long walk together. "You get credit, too,
you know, when you deserve
no such thing."

"It's strange," he agreed, as the glorious light
from the west swept across the heavens.
"This, for instance." He and Mrs. God
watched a great flock of starlings
rising and falling as one, a murmuration,

a miraculous enfolding at the day's end,
the movement of thousands of individuals
with a single mind. So it seemed.
"And yet," said God, "the starling
is not a pleasant bird."

Happy Birthday

It was God's birthday, but he had
completely lost track of his age.
So he said.

Mrs. God suggested they add days
to the year to prevent such
rapid aging

"as long as they're during the summer,"
whereas God felt the best approach
was to pad

days one loved with extra hours.
Sadly, people on earth were already
manufacturing wristwatches

especially the Swiss, the Germans,
and calendars had been built
into the very stone.

"Ah, well, we missed our moment,"
God said, stirring clouds over the sea
with his fingertip,

then watching them spin off and unspool
like ice skaters gliding in a stillness
immune to time.

A Sign

At the March for Science on Earth Day, 2017

"What did it say?" God asked.

"Well, first I should describe the day,"
Mrs. God replied. "It reminded me of creation,
an early tender morning, pure light,
the air thin, and every atom
unclaimed, simple...remember?"

"I think that's because there was no past."

"Exactly. Nothing had accumulated.
No old shoes or out of date bifocals in a tangle.
In those times we were still discussing
whether the chicken should lay the egg, or
whether the egg would need to hatch first, until
you thought of simultaneity.

God smiled, the most fluid of all his expressions.

"Anyway," Mrs. God continued, "people were
walking through the city. Sometimes they passed
through the deep purple shadows of tall buildings.
You could see them shiver, and the youngest
clung to their mothers. Then they emerged

into the light, and their arms opened
like the wings of sunning ravens. Many simply
walked, silent, happy to be among their kind,
and others carried signs on sticks."

"Why? What was this march about?"

"Well oddly enough, it was about
the value of the homo sapiens' ability to reason,
and honestly, I felt validated.
We spent a lot of time working on that."

"We were too good to them."

"No, no! Well...maybe. Anyway, one woman
who had a child at her side and another
developing under her heart held up a sign
that read: "What if Heaven and Earth
were the same place?"

God was silent.
"I know," said Mrs. God.
"She phrased it as a question?" he asked,
reaching for Mrs. God's hand.

The Bright Side

God was getting old,
but he'd been this way forever,
Mrs. God said. He always claimed
he liked Earth better "back then."

"It's hard, I know."
She sat beside him,
just beyond the water's reach.
"I prefer circles to lines," said God.
"Well," she half-smiled,
"We are all entitled to our preferences."

What was age but weariness?
A shortening of the stride,
non-organic pain, low clouds
that lacked definition, but not duration,
like a sheet of steel.

Best to sit quietly, Mrs. God knew,
because very soon he would say,
"And yet..."

ACKNOWLEDGMENTS

Grateful acknowledgment is made to the following publications in which poems first appeared:

*Upstree*t: "Mrs. God"
"Business"
"Genesis, Cont."
"First Love"

Freshwater Review:
"The Impulse to Create"
"Intelligent Design"

Rival Gardens: New and Selected Poems by permission of the University of Nebraska Press. Copyright 2016 by the Board of Regents of the University of Nebraska:

"Mrs. God"
"Genesis, Cont."
"Day of Rest"
"Business"
"First Love"

About the Author

Connie Wanek was born in Wisconsin, raised
in New Mexico, and lived for many years in Duluth,
MN, raising two children, gardening, canoeing, and
working at the Duluth Public Library.

Made in the USA
Columbia, SC
12 August 2018